ABOVE LOS ANGELES

by Robert Cameron

*A Collection of Nostalgic and Contemporary
Aerial Photographs of Greater Los Angeles*

Cameron and Company, San Francisco, California

Such a book as this does not reach publication without more than the usual amount of cooperation from many people. So, for their encouragement and expertise I thank the following:

And especially pilots:

Dale Berry, Bill Evans, Klaus Hense, Nick Kopanke, Tony Moreno, Darrell Ness, Bryan Roland, Steve Sirk, Tom Vusovich.

Blimp Pilots: Corky Balanger, Joel Chamberlain
John Crayton, Tom Matus, Nick Nicolary

Acknowledgement for Research Assistance is made to:

Hatfield History of Aeronautics, Northrop University
National Aeronautics and Space Administration, Ames Research Center
Security Pacific National Bank Historical Collection
Spence Collection, University of California at Los Angeles
Cabrillo Marine Museum

Cameron & Company
543 Howard Street
San Francisco, California 94105

Library of Congress Catalog Number: 76-2857
Above Los Angeles ISBN 0-918684-03-X
© 1980 by Robert W. Cameron and Company, Inc. All rights reserved.

First Printing, 1976
Second Printing, 1977
Third Printing, 1978
Fourth Printing, 1979
Fifth Printing, 1980
Sixth Printing, 1981
Seventh Printing, 1981
Eighth Printing, 1984

Book design by
Jane Olaug Kristiansen

Color Processing by G. P. Color
Typography by Reeder Typesetting
Color Separations and Printing by Dai Nippon, Tokyo, Japan

Hatsuro Aizawa, Robert Bredimus, David Hatfield, Michael Murphy, John Olguin, Anthony Orme, PhD, Peter Pascal, Don Piccard, Victor Plukas, Thomas Pochari, Carol Thares, Tom Wilhelm, Robert Wormhoudt, and Leonard Zuras.

TABLE OF CONTENTS

Introduction to
ABOVE LOS ANGELES
by Art Seidenbaum

What you have in your hands is a remarkable perspective on one of the world's most ill-defined and surprisingly beautiful regions, a ticket to ride above Los Angeles by helicopter and NASA U-2 and Goodyear blimp to see Southern California in all its sprawling wonder, in all that glorious stretch of natural and human imagination from ocean to stark desert.

Bob Cameron here gives us the opportunity to press our noses at the window of where we live: To look down the coast on a clear day. To see the mountains as the great parentheses that set off several sections of a city. To compare the historic aerial photographs of yesterday with the huge steel punctuation marks of today's skyline. To prove how hard we play, how brilliantly we light the night, how arrogantly we reshaped the earth. Suddenly the freeways emerge as spectacular sculpture. For once, the city is comprehensible. For native and newcomer, Los Angeles is no longer a blur of one-liners overlaid upon each other by near-sighted nightclub comedians, but is instead a site of spectacular sharpness and focus and clarity.

Cameron has hand-held this project for some three years. He is his own photographer, publisher, and archivist. And the result is his own vision of a piece of turf that hardly knows horizons.

The eye wanders as the mind begins to understand. Los Angeles is the name of a city, a county, a whole destination at the lower left-hand corner of America. So the camera looks all the way to San Diego, zooms as far as Palm Springs and Santa Barbara, hovers at Laguna and pauses in Long Beach before pretending to cover Los Angeles. We realize we are not the anonymous occupants of several suburbs in search of a city, but the new kind of nomads who planted the desert even as we paved it and who added striking color wherever we came to camp.

I'm a prejudiced admirer, of course. I love Los Angeles for all its room — for the terrain that continues to defy development, for the empty sociological spaces that allow residents to draw their own life plans, for the general warmth that makes a buttoned-down body look ridiculous.

And I love being able to see things, for a little while, as king of the mountain.

Aerial photography allows the magical opportunity to rise above routine scale, climb out and beyond our five-or-six-foot appreciation of the universe and embrace the world as if we were first-time tourists from another planet. The thrill is not unlike the spiritual act of separating oneself from one's body and being able to observe without the limitations of skin.

Those of us who live in Los Angeles will then quickly realize what we can recognize. You may find your own red-tile roof breaking out of the ground cover in the Santa Monica mountains. You may put your own index finger on a Pasadena cul-de-sac and call it home. You may even see yourself in a specific section at the last Superbowl. But even those who are indeed first-time tourists will see Southern California more sensibly here than from Hollywood Boulevard or Laguna Beach or a movie-star map.

Not all of it is sizzling sunset or choreographed surf. The ugliness also sticks out from above: the rashes of poor design breaking over several swatches of the landscape; the Parchesi-board monotony of urban grid patterns; the leveling of hills which reduces spirit as well as sense of place.

And the honest traveler coming home across these pages will also remember how few flights looked like Cameron's over the years. Most of the time when we make our airborne approaches to Los Angeles, there's that great gray bag in the sky, dulling the daylight or dimming the glow at night. "Above Los Angeles" tends to soar on the best days, generally refusing to look at the landfall when it's smeared with smog.

But who'd want to put smog on the coffee table or on the shelf with the art books? "Above Los Angeles" is a high-flying sister to "Above San Francisco," an earlier Cameron display of California from every altitude. The San Francisco book looks beautiful, but it looks easy by comparison. The Bay Area is so neatly sliced by water. The City with its funny downtown pyramid is such an obvious focal point. Capturing Los Angeles is a much more elusive chore because the borders are so indefinite, because the tall brush hides such a diversity of species.

My original love affair with Los Angeles was the uncritical love of a convert. I'd come from New York, where everyone knew his or her place and millions of them didn't like it. The Southern California basins brimmed with optimism by contrast.

I was a fieldhand for Life Magazine at the time, trying to send back words and pictures of Los Angeles that would help describe the sprawl and somehow make it containable in the minds of eastern editors. When I later decided to stay in California and went to work for the Los Angeles Times, my love for Southern California became slightly more sophisticated. Now I was trying to describe the sprawl to people who live in it — and hope the residents could find themselves sitting in those paragraphs.

Finally, along came Bob Cameron with his picture-perfect platforms on top of the whole sun-streaked, canyon-pocked, water-kissed confusion. You will find elusive Los Angeles in the following pages, captured with extraordinary technological grace and exquisite hand-held care.

"Above Los Angeles" is nothing less than our largest family album shot by a most unusual professional, a portrait photographer from 40 to 14,000 feet, who knew exactly how to concentrate on our best sides and how to present our wrinkles in their most flattering light.

Shoreline

Looking over beautified offshore oil rigs toward the Queen Mary at sunset — Long Beach and Los Angeles harbors.

This small section of Malibu homes is the original "Colony."
At upper right can be seen the Hughes Research Center. 11

A ballgame is in progress beside Pepperdine University's Malibu Campus.

The Howard Hughes Glomar Explorer sits near the hangar that houses his "Spruce Goose" in Los Angeles Harbor.

The new J. Paul Getty Museum near Topanga Beach.

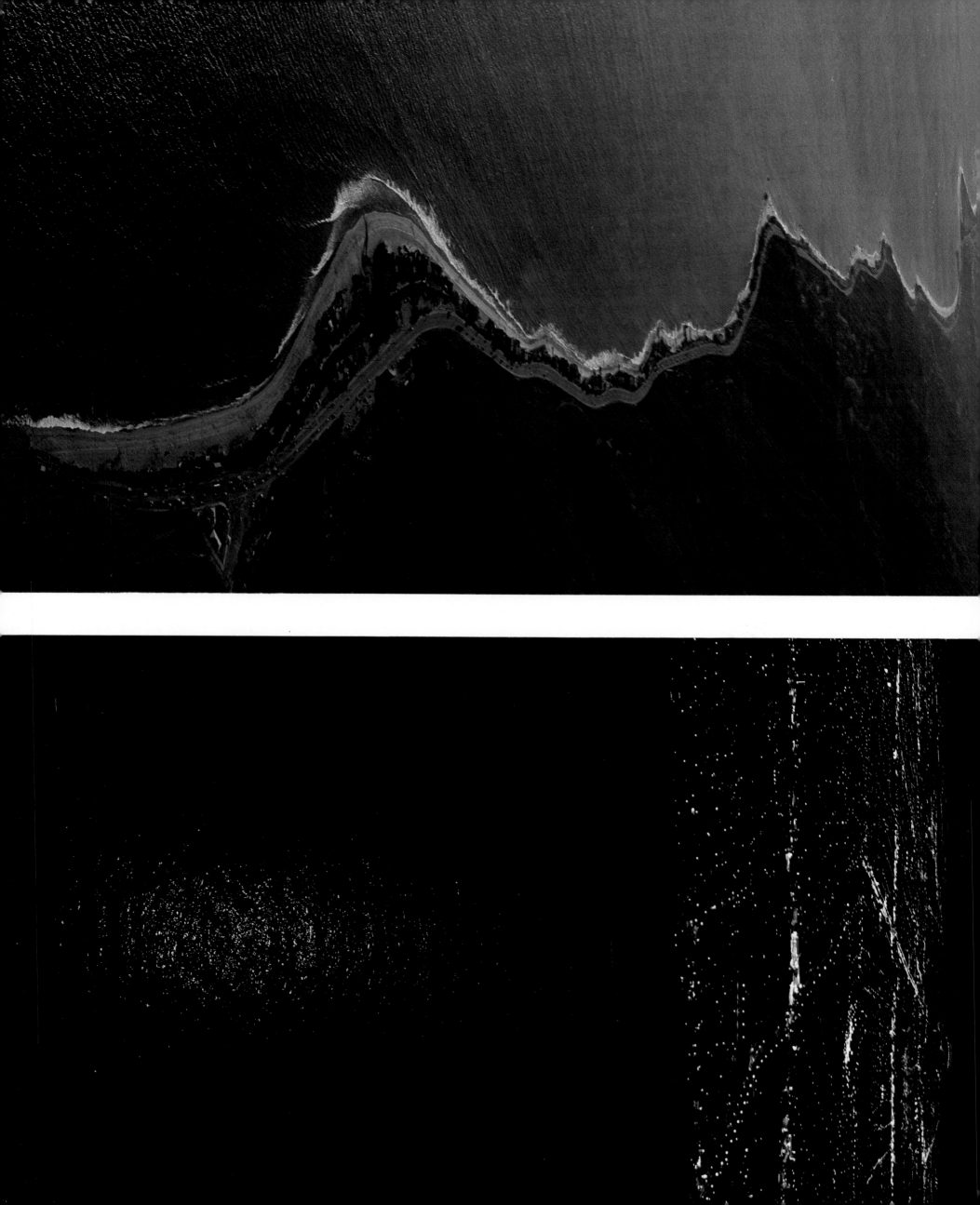

Sunset Boulevard terminates at the Pacific Coast Highway in Pacific Palisades. This was once known as Inceville, where Howard Ince built his movie studios in 1915.

The Pacific Coast Highway winds its way north to Santa Barbara. Moonlight on the ocean seen from the cruising blimp.

The artists' community of Venice lies near Marina del Rey. The bridges and canals were patterned after its Italian counterpart.

16

King Harbor Marina looking northeast. Hermosa Beach is at left.

17

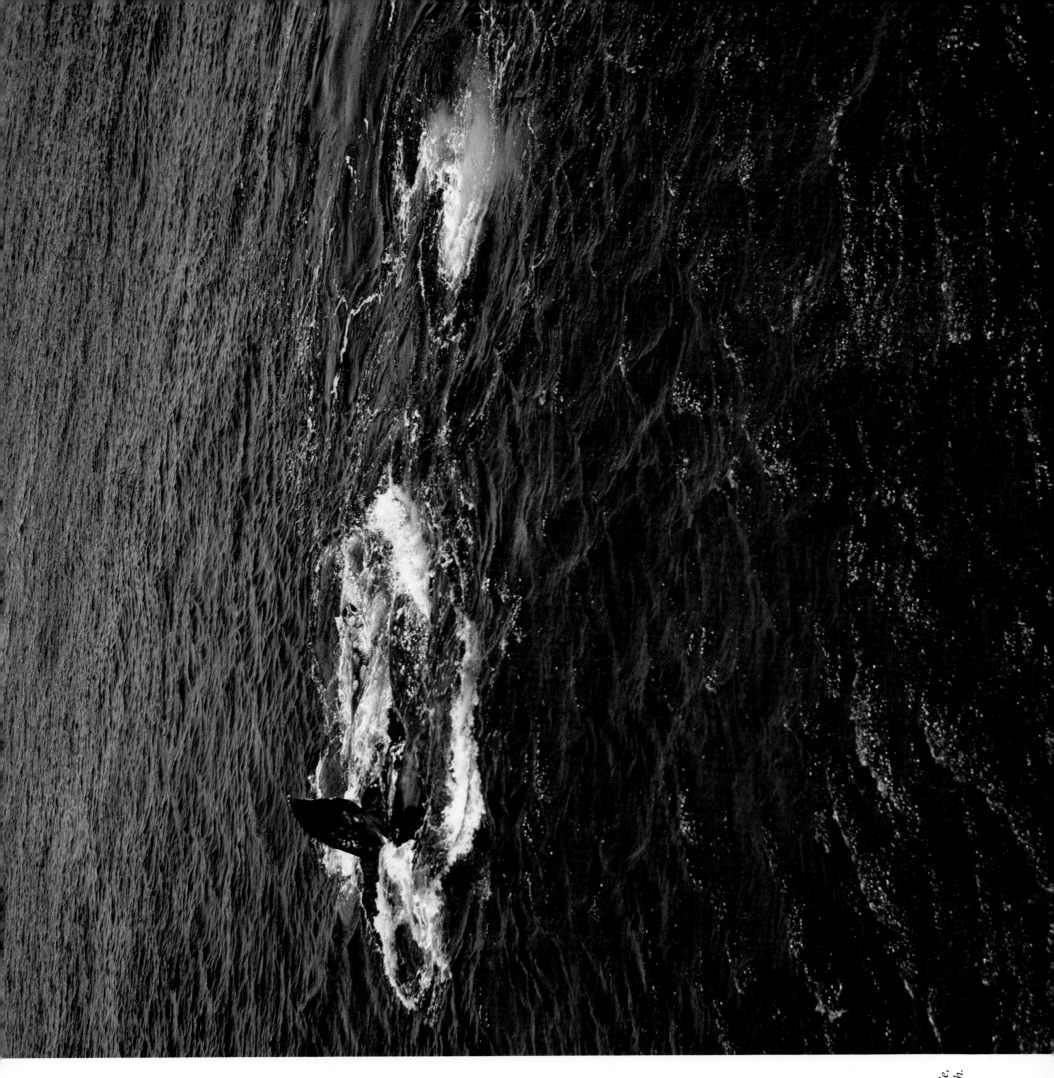

36,000 school children join the "Whale Watchers Club" every year as the migrating grey whales pass through the Catalina Channel on their way to Baja. Once down to less than 800 whales, the migration now involves in excess of 11,000.

Mating grey whales (female, two males) off Newport Beach.

Two views of Marina del Rey; its share of Los Angeles County's 98,000 boats makes it the largest marina of its kind in the world.

A geological fault creases Palos Verdes.

Palos Verdes looking northeast toward the city. Building codes once stipulated red-tiled roofs.

The disappearing sun makes a silhouette of Terminal Island.

Point Fermin from the beautiful belly of the blimp.

The Queen Mary, by night and by day. She has now been permanently docked at
Long Beach. She once set Atlantic speed records and is now a museum and hotel.

26

Newport Beach looking towards snow-capped peaks in the distance. In the bay is Lido Isle.

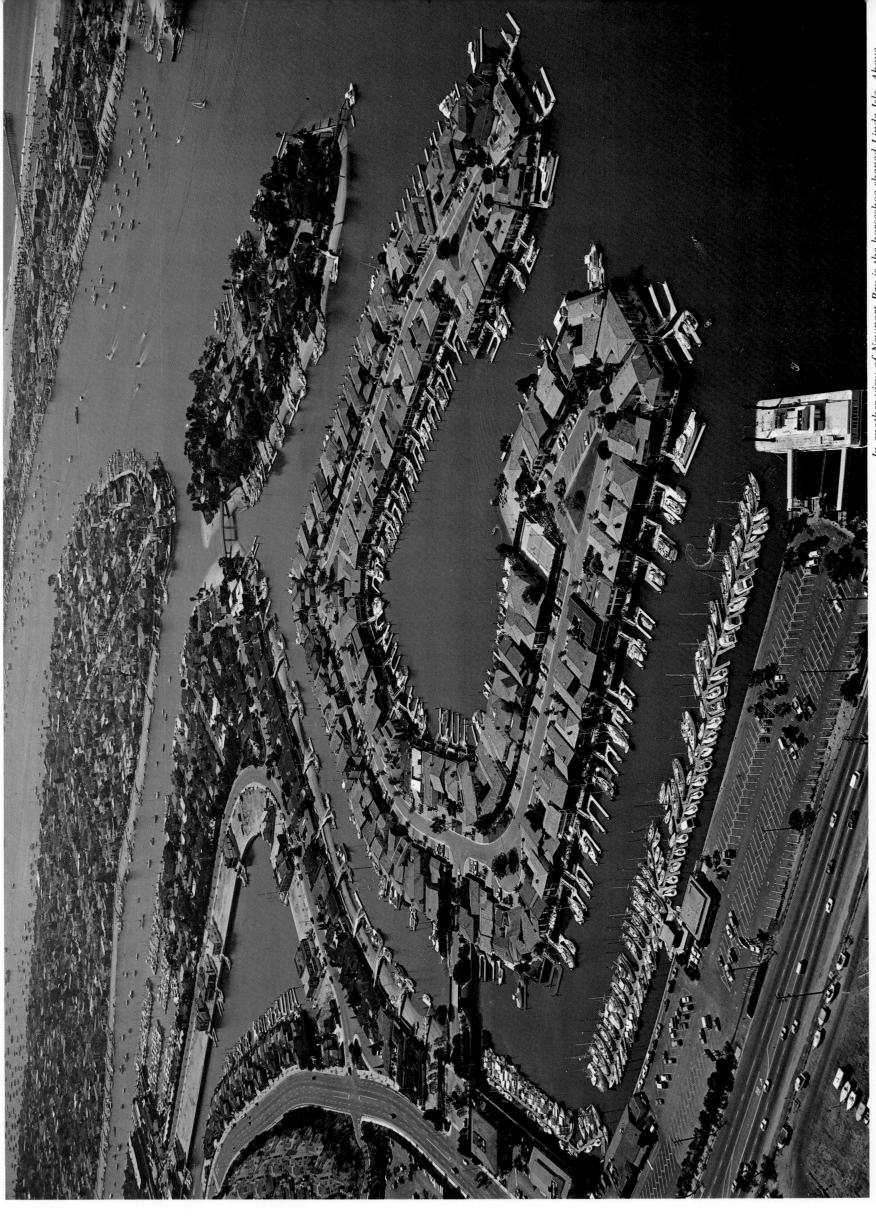

In another view of Newport Bay is the horseshoe-shaped Linda Isle. Above it, Harbor Isle, and at top, Balboa Island as we look toward the ocean.

Balboa, an island of luxury in Newport Bay.

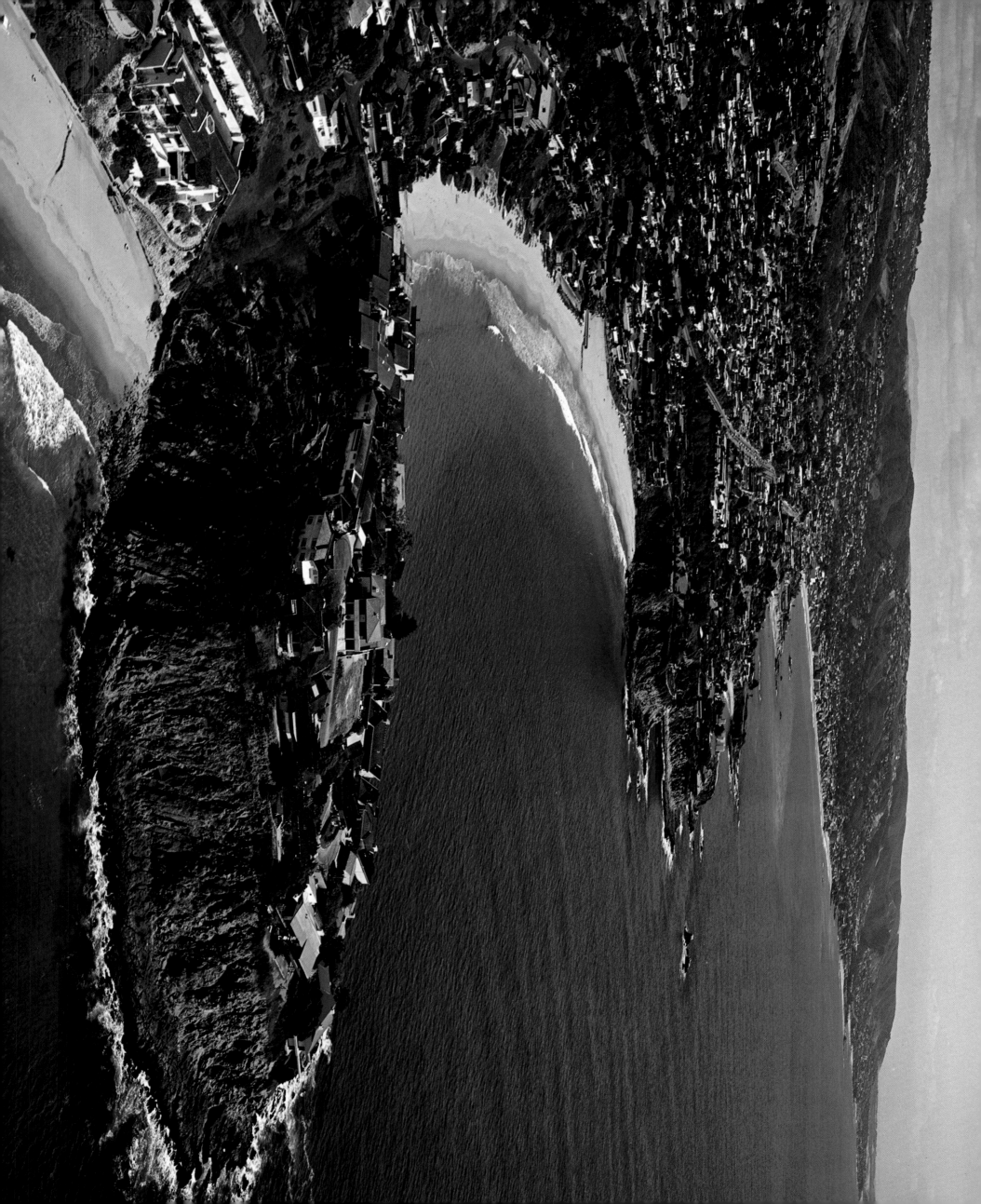

*Emerald Bay, north
of Laguna Beach.*

San Pedro Hill at dusk.

Dana Point, named for Richard
Henry Dana, author of TWO
YEARS BEFORE THE MAST.
He first touched here in 1834.

A lone figure walks the
beach at San Clemente.

Avalon on Catalina Island. At upper left, the large round Avalon Ballroom was famous for big bands in the thirties. 37

A dolphin family cruises the Catalina Channel.

This photograph of the Southern California Exposition in 1904 was made from a balloon. (below) The same scene today: At left is the Los Angeles Coliseum, built for the 1932 Olympics, and now the home of the Los Angeles Rams. The Sports Arena is at lower right; behind is Exposition Park and the University of Southern California campus.

Then and Now

Beverly Hills Hotel, 1920.

Beverly Hills Hotel, today.

Pasadena from a balloon in 1900.

42

In San Marino, the Henry E. Huntington Art Gallery and Library is set in Gardens that are world famous. Pasadena is seen in the distance.

Twentieth Century Fox Studios in 1937.

Twentieth Century Fox Studios today: At center, Century
City has replaced the oil rigs in the opposite photograph.

Warner Brothers (First National) Studios in Burbank, 1928.

The Burbank Studios in foreground, the San Fernando Valley stretches northwest.

Westwood in 1929. Construction of UCLA (at top) began in 1926.

Westwood today. At right center, additions to UCLA Medical Center are under construction.

The intersection of Wilshire and Fairfax in 1921. There were three airfields at this location: Chaplin, DeMille, and Rogers. Motorists have driven out for an air show. The La Brea Tar Pits are at right of the oil rigs seen at top.

Wilshire and Fairfax today: The Los Angeles County Art Museum at right center is adjacent to the La Brea Tar Pits. At upper left is Park La Brea residential complex.

\At Mines Field, biplanes race past the grandstand at the 1928 National Air Races.

(below) In 1929, motorists have driven out from the city to see the Graf Zeppelin at Mines Field (now Los Angeles International Airport.) It had just flown non-stop from Tokyo.

(opposite page) Los Angeles International Airport looking toward the ocean.

The Beverly Speedway at the intersection of Santa Monica and Wilshire Boulevards in 1922. Close inspection shows that there were parking problems even then.

54

Downtown Beverly Hills today: Santa Monica and Wilshire Boulevards intersect at left.

In 1923, the San Fernando Valley was largely agricultural.

Today, with the population over a million and growing, the Valley has become an urban empire in its own right.

The construction of the Rose Bowl nears completion in 1922.

UCLA upsets Ohio State in this Rose Bowl Game. In the distant foothills of the San Gabriel Mountains are the Jet Propulsion Laboratories.

Looking north along the Pacific coastline over Hermosa and Manhattan Beaches in 1925.

This southern section of the Pacific Coast shoreline presents a very different look today.

A Vought biplane is silhouetted against the Navy dirigible "Shenandoah." The "Hollywoodland" sign is faintly discernible at upper left.

The Hollywood Hills, Lake Hollywood at left, and the "Hollywood" sign atop Mt. Lee.

Signal Hill Oil Fields in 1929.

A few separated oil pumps still deck Signal Hill today.

Lockheed Aircraft at Burbank in 1928.

Hollywood-Burbank Airport Terminal is at lower right; across the runways are the Lockheed Buildings at this location today.

Many important motion pictures were premiered at the Fox Carthay Circle Theater, seen here in 1921.

Today, modern buildings have replaced the theater; San Vicente Boulevard and Olympic Boulevard intersect at upper right.

C.

D.

a.
Louis Paulhan, flying his Farman biplane, set an altitude record of 4,165 feet.

b.
This composite photo shows some of 200,000 spectators who attended the world's first International Air Meet at Dominguez Field in January, 1910.

c.
This event was billed as "The Great Dirigible Race" between Roy Knabenshue and Lincoln Beachey.

d.
The Examiner balloon was probably flown by Knabenshue.

California State College, Dominguez Hills, now occupies the site.

Will Rogers' ranch near Santa Monica in 1929. It became a popular polo field.

Looking north toward the Santa Monica Mountains, we see what is now Will Rogers State Park. Polo is still played here.

Santa Monica Beach, 1900.

Santa Monica Beach today: The red building at center of
preserved Santa Monica Pier houses a merry-go-round.

The Palm Springs Airport under snow-capped peaks in 1946.

Looking up the desert over a Palm Springs golf course in mid-winter.

Downtown

*Los Angeles' new Convention Center and skyscrapers dominate this scene.
City Hall in background was for many years the tallest building here.*

79

Looking west past City Hall along Civic Center Mall toward the Music Center and the Department of Water and Power. 81

At lower right is the old Town House, now the Sheraton West Hotel. Wilshire Boulevard makes its way past Lafayette Park toward MacArthur Park Lake on its way downtown.

The new Hotel Bonaventure complex rises among skyscrapers downtown.

At lower left center is Los Angeles' Original Plaza below shops on Olvera Street. Union Station is at right; the white building with heliports on the roof is the Main Downtown Post Office.

Day and night views of one of the world's busiest and most compli-cated traffic interchanges. Sometimes referred to as "The Stack" in downtown Los Angeles, it is used by 350,000 vehicles per day.

County and state Museums ring the
Rose Garden at Exposition Park.

These are the Watts Towers; fifteen in
all, the tallest rises to 104 feet. Made
from bits and pieces of this and that,
they took many years to construct.

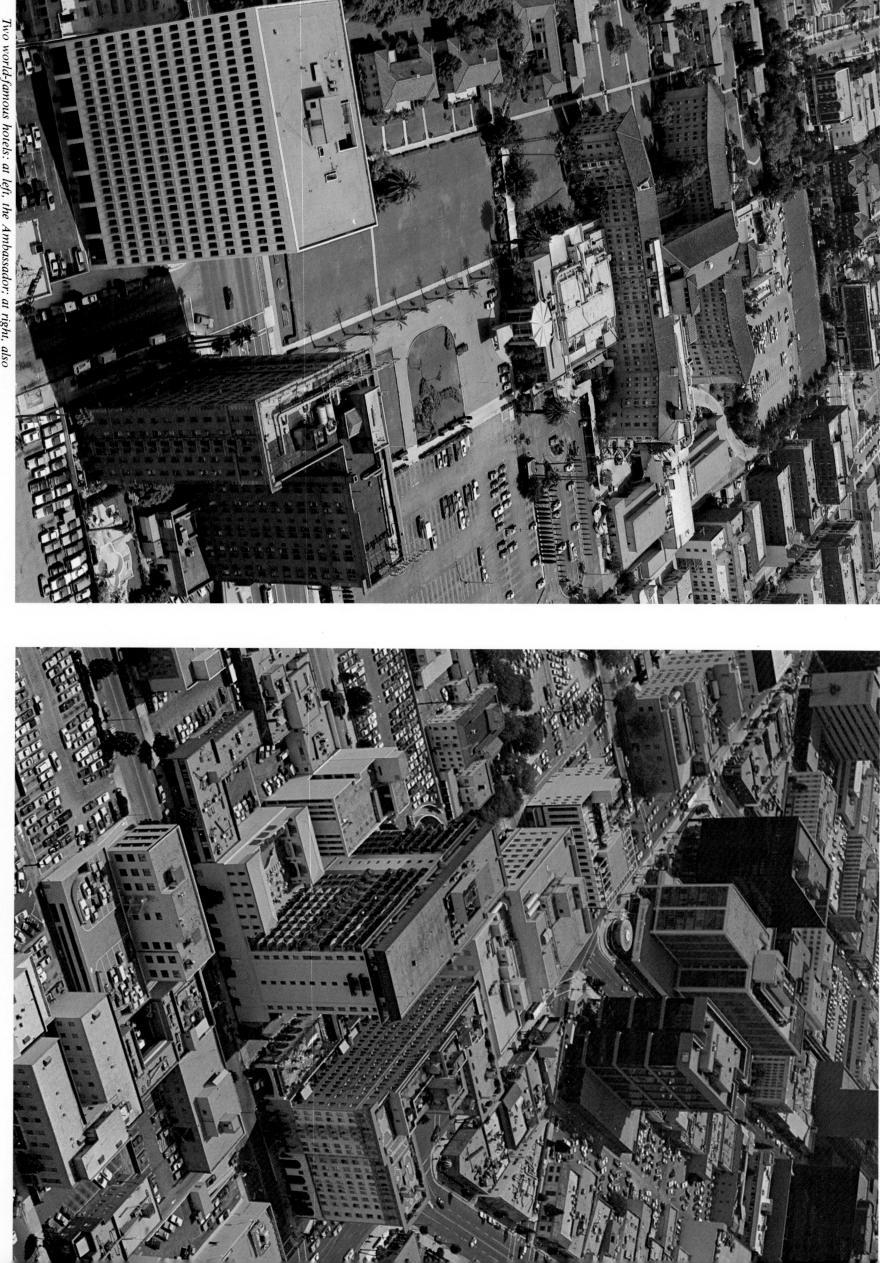

Two world-famous hotels: at left, the Ambassador; at right, also on Wilshire Boulevard, several miles west is the Beverly Wilshire.

(opposite page) The eye of CBS's Television City looks right toward Farmer's Market with downtown in the distance.

Environs

The Ventura Freeway heads west past Forest Lawn Cemetery. From bottom to top are seen: Disney Studios, St. Joseph's Hospital, NBC Television Studios, the Burbank Studios, and Universal City.

Residential canyons looking south toward Westwood and Century City.

Beverly Glen goes south past Stone Canyon Reservoir.

The Bel Air Hotel and Bel Air Country Club.

Looking southeast toward downtown from the Santa Monica Mountains.

These two photographs of residential Beverly Hills show the greatest
concentration of homes of film stars and other celebrities.

*The famous Hollywood inter-
section of Sunset and Vine at
lower left. Vine continues north
past Hollywood Boulevard and
the circular Capitol Records
Tower to the Hollywood Freeway.*

*Mann's Chinese Theatre (formerly
Graumann's), a venerable institution
on Hollywood Boulevard.*

*Paramount Studios at Melrose
and Gower.*

MGM Studios in Culver City.

Universal Studios, Sheraton Universal Hotel, Universal tour grounds and
movie backlot, Lakeside Country Club and Burbank Studios at left center.

The Ventura Freeway goes past Glendale toward Pasadena.
The San Bernardino Mountains are in the distance.

A part of Hollywood's Sunset Strip.

Downtown Hollywood looking northwest through the Cahuenga Pass.

The myriad lights of Los Angeles from the air at night extend to distances seen nowhere else. This shows only a part of its 463 square miles.

106

The Huntington Hotel in San Marino. Downtown Pasadena is in the background.

At top, the sun over the Pacific Ocean reflects on the northern slope of the Santa Monica Mountains. Lake Calabasas is in foreground.

Rocketdyne Test Area in Simi Hills at the western end of the San Fernando Valley.

New automobiles, which often arrive by water, flow from distribution centers such as this. The number of our automobiles, trucks, motorcycles, and trailers was 5,003,796 at last count.

*A full moon climbs above Ventura
Boulevard in the San Fernando
Valley. A snow-covered Mount
Baldy can be seen on the horizon.*

*Hillside homes above Encino
Reservoir, looking toward the
San Fernando Valley.*

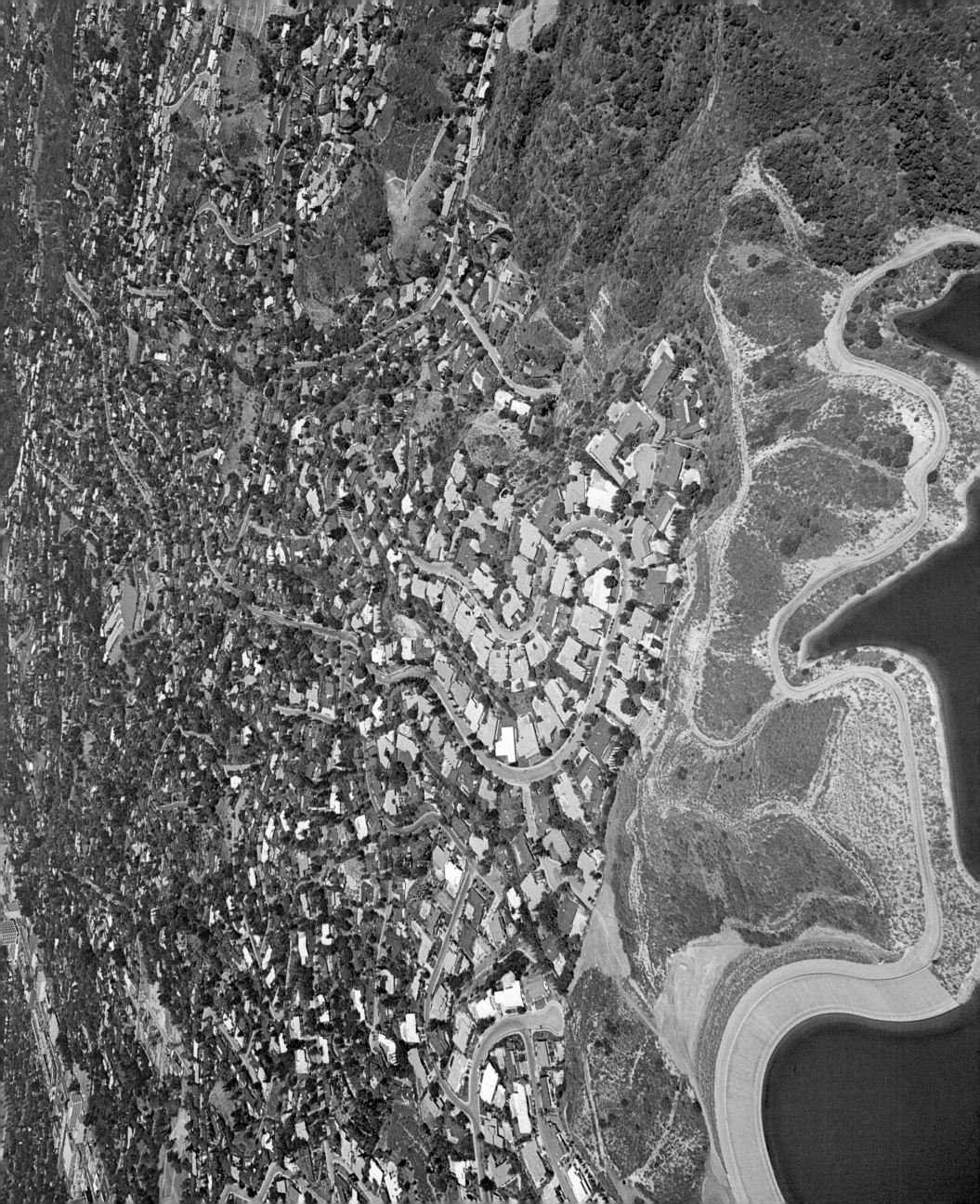

Space Division of Rockwell International in Downey. On the concrete slab at lower right are the insignia of all the Sky-Labs and Apollo rockets fabricated here. 115

Redistribution of everything and anything you can imagine takes place at Swap Meets such as this one near Torrance.

Strawberry pickers animate this geometric agricultural design in Orange County.

Evening commuters traveling to and from the San Fernando Valley on the San Diego Freeway.

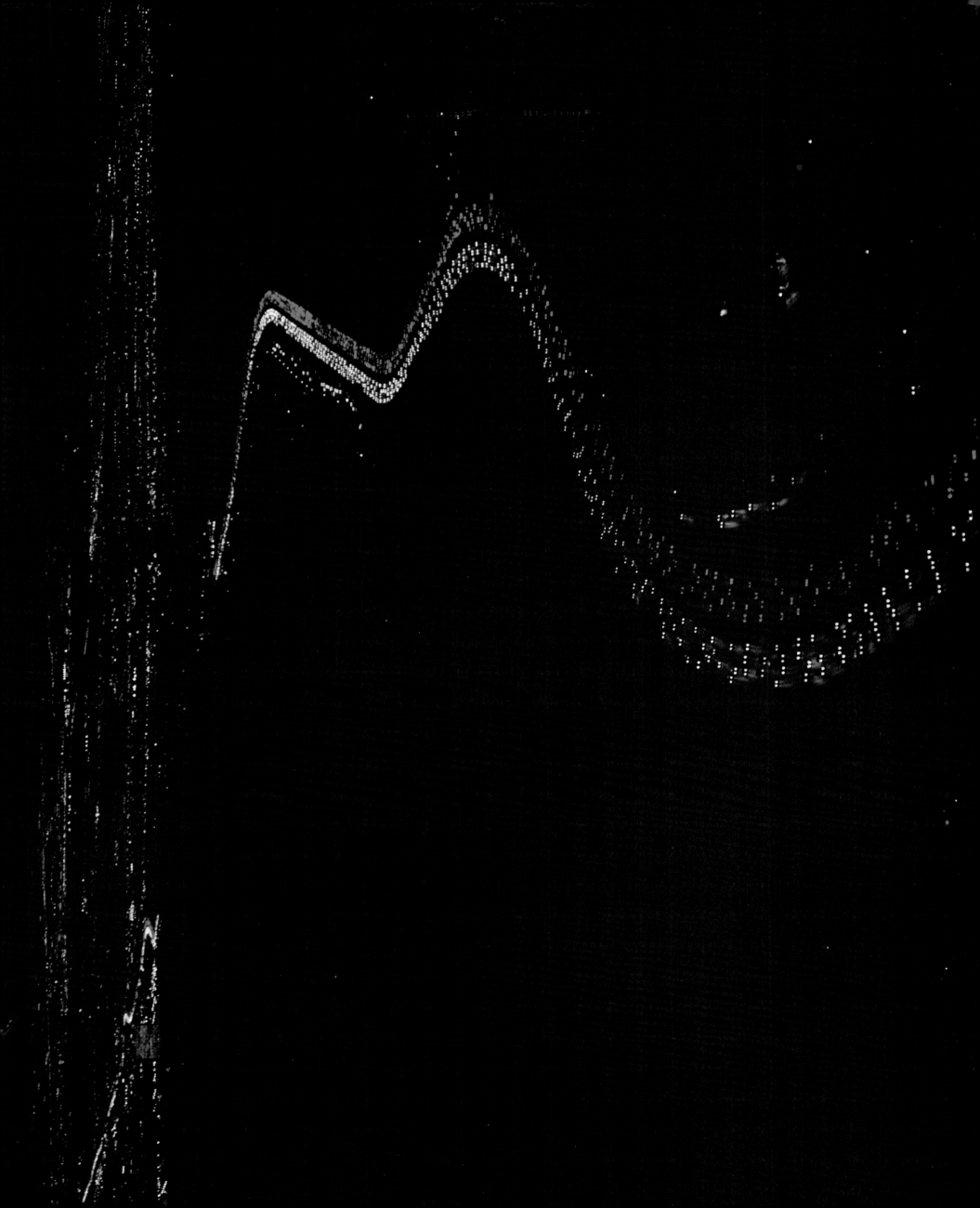

University of California at Irvine sits on the former 93,000 acre Irvine Ranch.

Mission San Juan Capistrano;
founded, 1776.

Sports and Entertainment

Sixteen Formula One racing cars on the final day of the United States Grand Prix West, held on the streets of downtown Long Beach.

Hollywood Park Racetrack at Inglewood. Sports Forum is seen at top.

Santa Anita Racetrack in Arcadia has a very special setting —
on this day there was snow on the San Gabriel Mountains above.

Griffith Park Observatory sits above the Greek Theater on Los Feliz Boulevard.

The Hollywood Bowl must be photographed empty; no planes are allowed near when a concert is in progress.

Proof of tennis' burgeoning popularity is in foreground. Wilshire Country Club is seen above.

Looking south over the Los Angeles Country Club toward Century City.

Just south of Century City lies the Hillcrest Country Club.

127

Brentwood Golf and Country Club in Santa Monica. The Pacific and Malibu can be seen in the distance.

The Gallery surrounds the 18th green on the final day of the Los Angeles Open at the Riviera Country Club.

The Los Angeles Coliseum hosted the Super Bowl in 1973.

132

On opening night, the Dodgers were rained out for the first time in 13 years.

The California Angels' opening night at Anaheim's "Big A."

A Saturday morning finds eight Little League teams playing their hearts out at Westminster.

Lawn Bowls on the shoreline green at Laguna Beach.

More than 1,000,000 people watch the
Tournament of Roses Parade make its
way down Colorado Avenue every
January 1 in Pasadena.

The mist-shrouded peaks of the
San Bernardino Mountains surround
Lake Arrowhead.

The first gala fireworks of the Disneyland season.

Knott's Berry Farm near Buena Park.

Busch Gardens in Van Nuys, in addition to its other attractions, boasts a "Brewery Tour."

Marineland near Abalone Cove on Palos Verdes.

A few of the thousands of surfers along the Pacific shoreline. These are enjoying the waves near Newport Beach.

The Los Angeles Zoo in Griffith's Park; it is adjacent to the Harding Municipal Golf Course, seen at top.

Ballooning is an ever-increasing sport in the area. Here and on the next two pages, the preparations and take-off from a Buena Park schoolyard for an overland race.

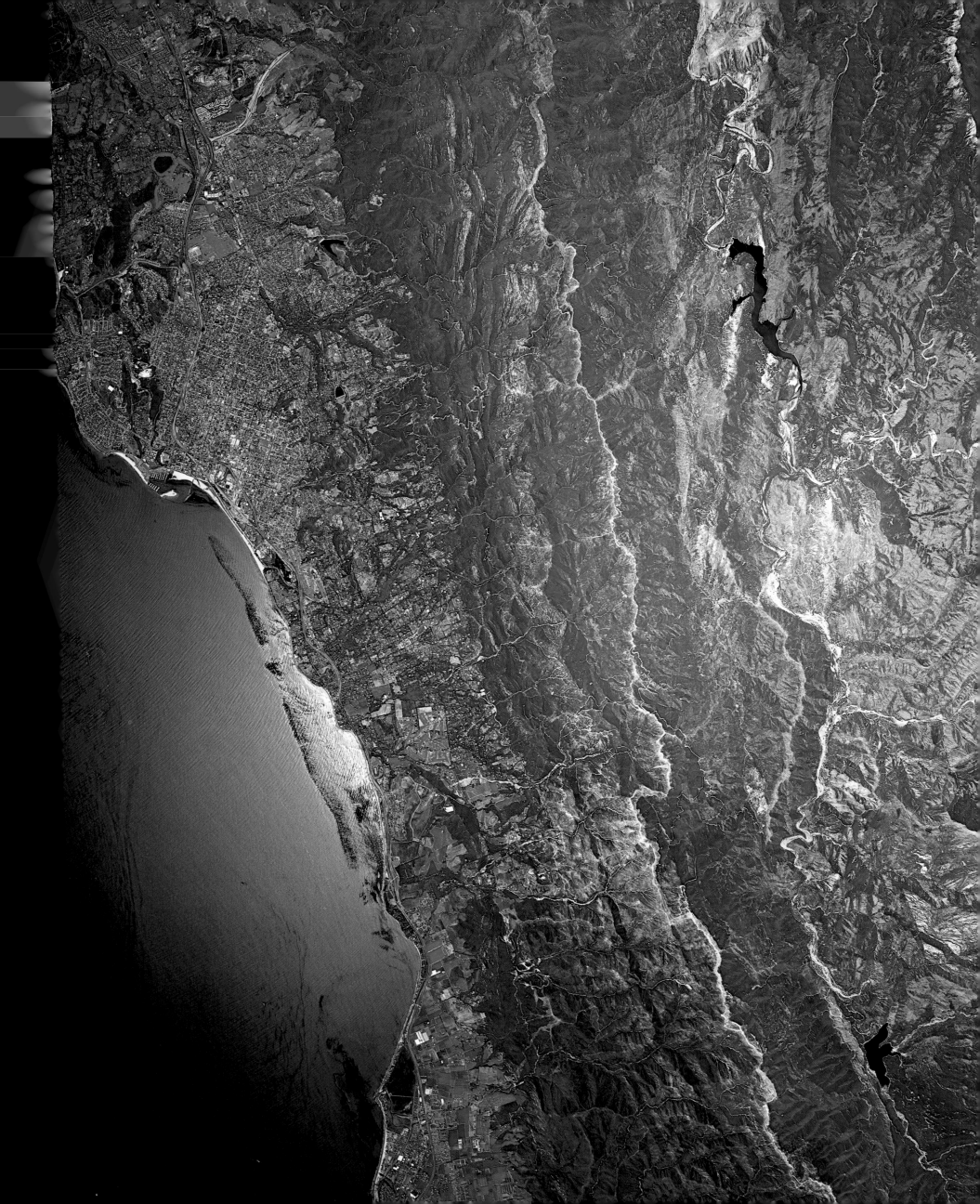

High Above

The amazing photographs on the next eleven pages are taken from the U-2 Observation Plane under the auspices of NASA. The definition and resolution in these pictures taken from 65,000 feet demonstrate the technical perfection possible when experimentation, knowledge, and implementation are combined. At left, an infra-red photograph shows Santa Barbara and the coastline heading south toward Los Angeles.

Central Los Angeles (again on infra-red film). A point of reference near the center is Dodger Stadium; looking north and near the top is the Rose Bowl.

Our neighbor, San Diego, also in infra-red. La Jolla at lower left sticks out into the Pacific. Mission Bay is at center. Point Loma is the finger pointing to the right, and above the finger, Coronado.

This high shot of the Santa Monica
Mountains is again in infra-red.
Note that the fairways of the golf
courses, being green, show up as
red. At lower left on the Pacific
shoreline is Marina del Rey.

This faraway look on regular
color film was chosen because it
shows the basin, the mountains,
and the desert beyond.

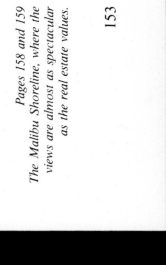

153

*Pages 154 and 155
Starting from the ocean at left are
tiny white specks which turn out
to be planes that have just taken
off from LAX at center. Hollywood Park is at right with
thousands of homes in between.*

*Pages 156 and 157
Looking from left to right: the
San Diego Freeway, the hills of
Bel-Air, and the community of
Westwood; the intersection of
Wilshire and Santa Monica
Boulevards at Beverly Hills, in
center, the Sunset Strip and the
Hollywood Hills. The geometry at
lower right is Park La Brea
Complex.*

*Pages 158 and 159
The Malibu Shoreline, where the
views are almost as spectacular
as the real estate values.*

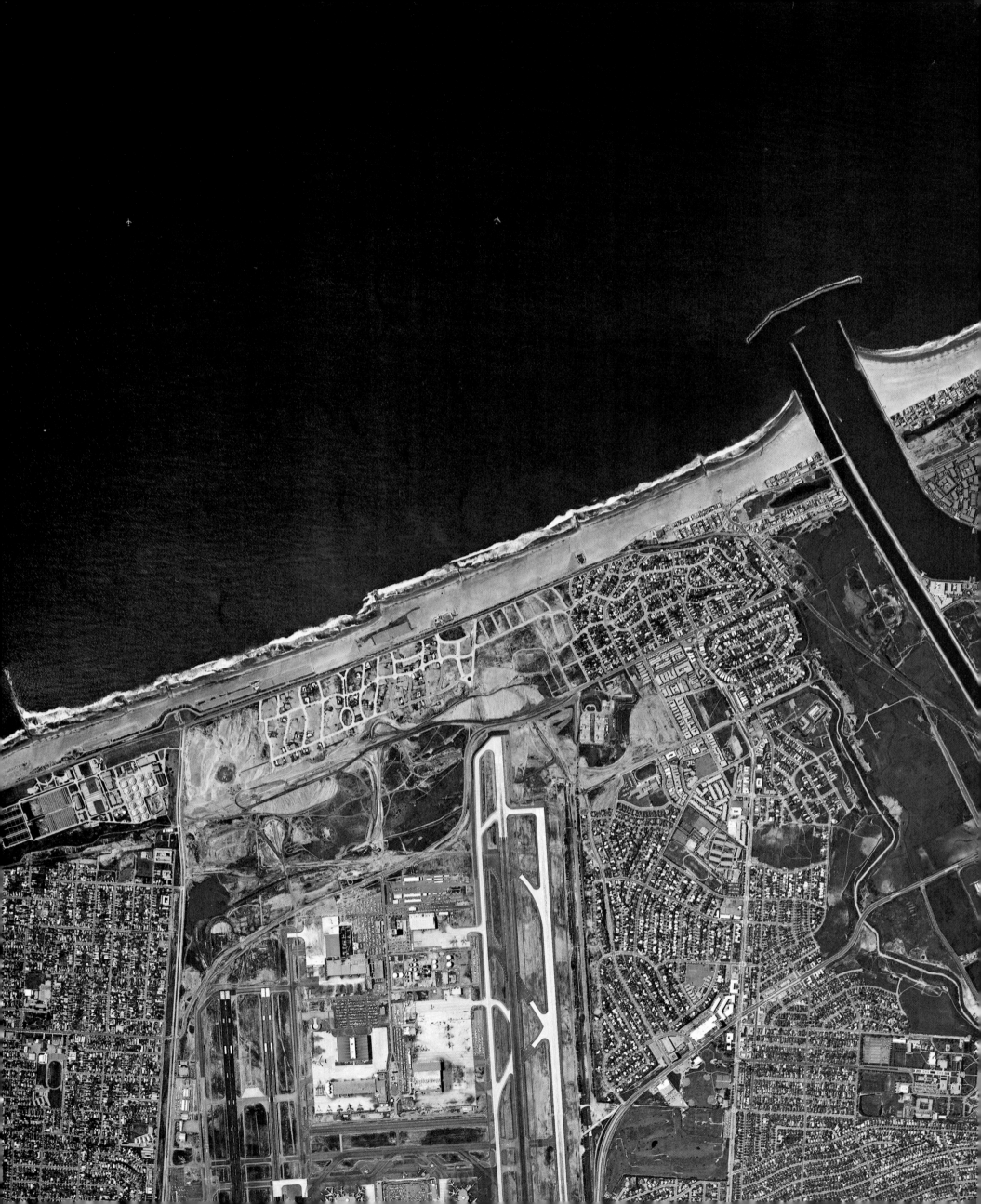

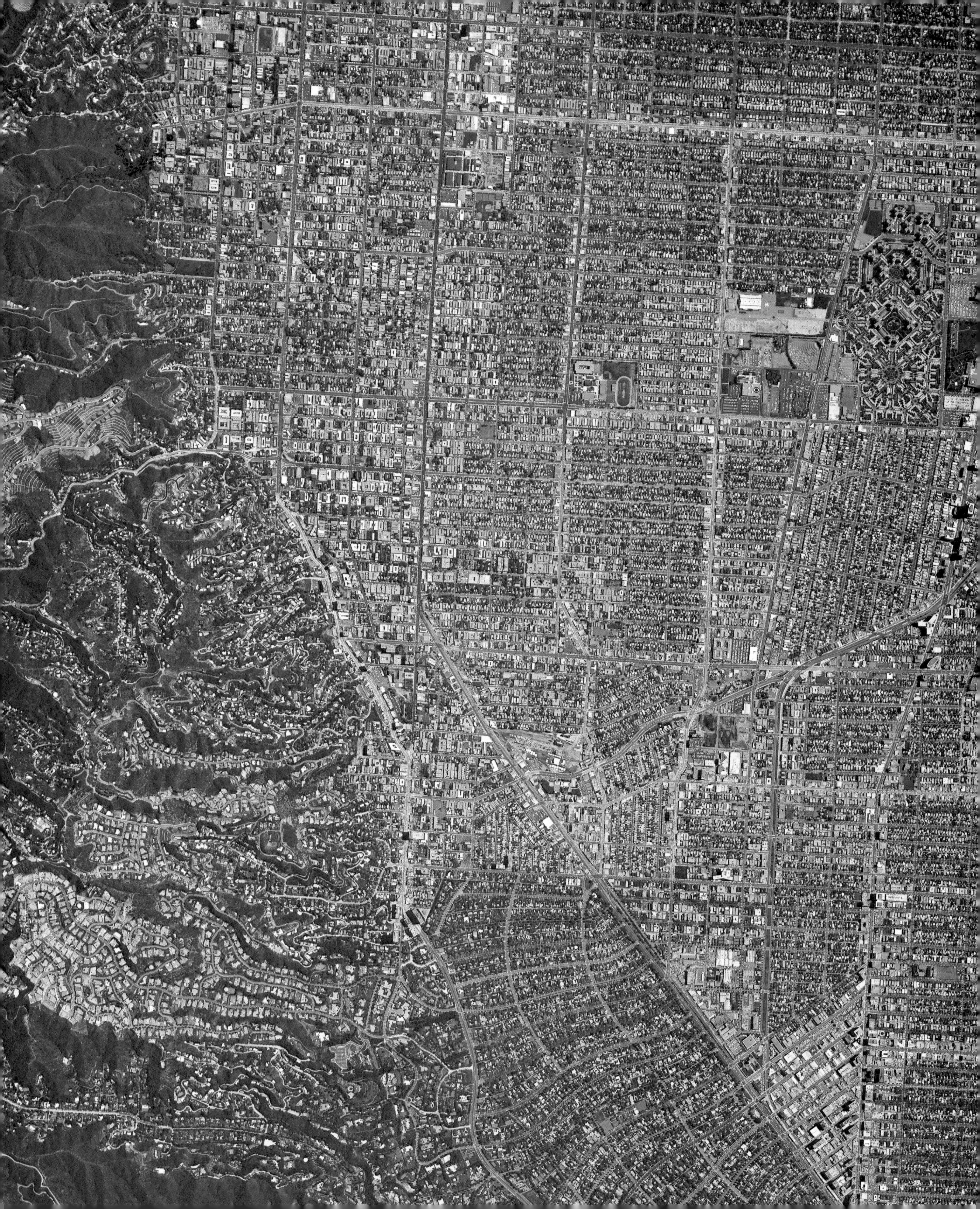

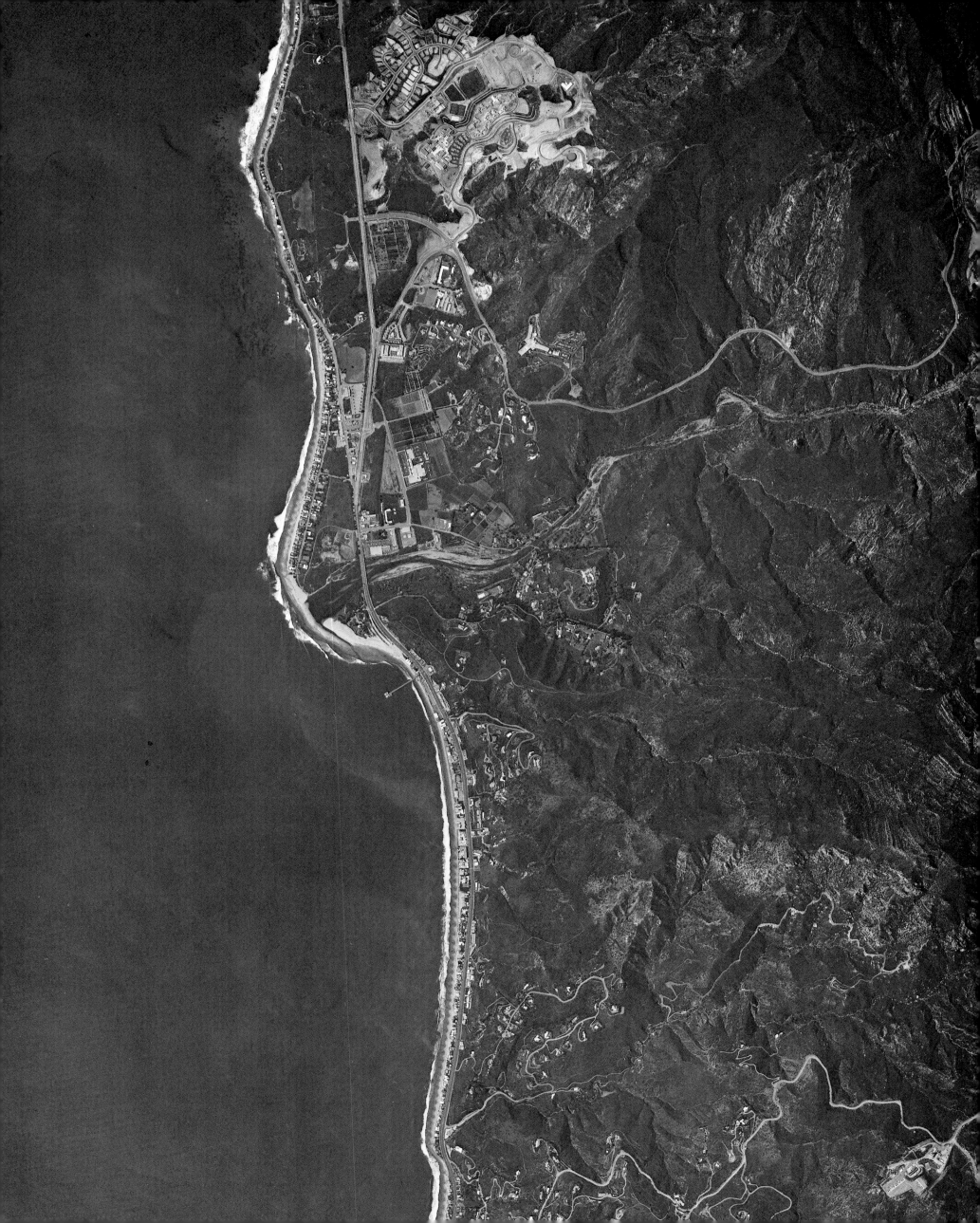